Clever Bird

Written by Charlie Chin
Illustrated by Oki Han

W9-AWC-741

CelebrationPress

An Imprint of ScottForesman
A Division of HarperCollinsPublishers

Long ago in China, there lived a man named Mo Chin. One day a rich farmer offered him a job. The farmer would pay him ten gold pieces if Mo Chin could work for one year without complaining.

The rich farmer had planned all along to trick Mo Chin. On the last day, he gave him boiled stones for dinner.

Mo Chin said he could not chew his food. The farmer said, "You are complaining. I owe you nothing."

Soon everyone had heard the story of what happened. The villagers said, "That greedy farmer needs to be taught a lesson."

So they bought a clever parrot and taught it to say, "Yes, of course."

Then they buried a sack of gold coins by a
tree in the forest near a flowing stream.

The next day, the farmer met Mo Chin walking with his bird. "Don't ask me for money," said the farmer. "Be gone!"

But Mo Chin just laughed and said, "Oh, I don't need your money. I have this wonderful bird. He can find gold coins."

"Prove it," said the greedy farmer.

11

They walked into the forest. Soon they reached a tree near the flowing stream. Mo Chin asked his bird, "Is this a good place to find gold?"

The bird said, "Yes, of course."

Mo Chin dug up the gold coins. The farmer shouted, "I will pay ten gold pieces for that bird!"

Mo Chin happily took the money and went home, and the farmer ran into the fields with the bird.

He asked, "Is this a good place to find gold?"

The bird said, "Yes, of course."

The farmer dug all day, but found nothing. He groaned, "Now Mo Chin has his gold. And I was greedy."

"Yes, of course!" said the bird.